DRAW 50 CREEPY CRAWLIES

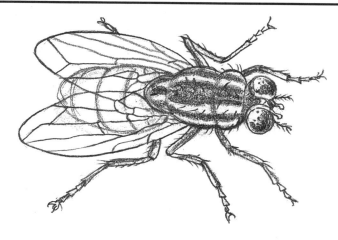

DRAW
50 CREEPY
CRAWLIES

LEE J. AMES
with
RAY BURNS

DOUBLEDAY

NEW YORK   LONDON   TORONTO   SYDNEY   AUCKLAND

PUBLISHED BY DOUBLEDAY
a division of Bantam Doubleday Dell Publishing Group, Inc.
666 Fifth Avenue, New York, New York 10103

DOUBLEDAY
and the portrayal of an anchor with a dolphin
are trademarks of Doubleday, a division of
Bantam Doubleday Dell Publishing Group, Inc.

Library of Congress Cataloging-in-Publication Data

Ames, Lee J.
Draw 50 creepy crawlies / Lee J. Ames with Ray Burns.—1st ed.
p.   cm.
Summary: Step-by-step instructions for drawing fifty different insects, spiders, and
other crawling or flying creatures.
1. Insects in art—Juvenile literature. 2. Animals in art—Juvenile literature. 3.
Drawing—Technique—Juvenile literature. [1. Insects in art. 2. Animals in art. 3.
Drawing—Technique.] I. Burns, Raymond, 1924– . II. Title. III. Title: Draw fifty
creepy crawlies.
NC783.A44 1991
743′.6—dc20   90-19396   CIP   AC

ISBN 0-385-41189-8
ISBN 0-385-41190-1 (lib. bdg.)

Thanks again, Ray,
for sharing with me your wonderful talent.
—L.J.A.

To Lee Ames,
a good friend these many years.
—R.B.

TO THE READER

This is number twenty in our "Draw 50" series. This is the twentieth time I've had the fun and privilege of showing you a way of creating drawings. This time it's the method used by Ray Burns and myself. Working with Ray, and bringing his unique talent to the book, made this a most delightful experience.

Ray is a top illustrator of our time. In your library and bookstore, you will find many books that have been enhanced by his talent. In black and white, in full color, from cartoons to fantasy to realism, from fairy tales to history to natural science, he has shown himself to be an expert. Thank you, Ray, for joining with me in this project!

When you start working, I would recommend you use clean white bond paper or drawing paper and a pencil with moderately soft lead (HB or No. 2). Keep a kneaded eraser (available at art supply stores) handy. Choose the creepy crawly you want to draw and then, very lightly and very carefully, sketch out the first step. Also very lightly and carefully, add the second step. As you go along, study not only the lines but the spaces between the lines. Size your first steps as closely as possible to the lines and the spaces in the book—not too large, not too small. Remember, the first steps must be constructed with the greatest care. A mistake here could ruin the entire drawing.

As you work, it's a good idea to hold a mirror to your sketch from time to time. The image in the mirror frequently shows distortion you might not have noticed otherwise.

In the book, new steps are printed darker than the previous steps. This is so they can be clearly seen. But you should keep your construction steps very light. Here's where the kneaded eraser can be useful. You can use it to lighten a pencil stroke that is too dark.

When you've completed all the steps, and when you're sure you have everything the way you want it, complete the drawing with firm, strong penciling. If you like, you can go over this with India ink (applied with a fine brush or pen), or a permanent fine-tipped ballpoint or felt-tipped marker. When your work is thoroughly dry, you can then use the kneaded eraser to clean out all the underlying pencil marks.

Always remember that even if your first attempts at drawing do not turn out the way you'd like, it's important to *keep trying.* Your efforts *will* eventually pay off and you'll be pleased by what you can accomplish.

I sincerely hope you will improve your drawing skills and have a great time working on these creepers and crawlers.

LEE J. AMES

TO THE PARENT OR TEACHER

In fourth grade, many years ago, we were given an assignment to draw something to honor President Lincoln's birthday. An immediate competition developed among the four or five class artists. Which of us could draw the best portrait of Honest Abe?

We, of course, would not agree that any other one of us did the best. Our pride led each of us to consider himself the winner. Today I couldn't honestly make the judgment call that mine deserved to be number one, but I did learn something that ultimately resulted in the "Draw 50" books.

I learned the importance of peer approval. The encouragement given to us artists by the rest of the class and the praise we gave one another was heady inspiration. Most of the group went on to become successful professionals.

All the drawings of Abraham Lincoln that the class artists made were copied from other sources. This despite general disapproval of "copying." We copied from the Lincoln penny; from a five-dollar bill; from a calendar; and from sale advertisements in the newspaper. We copied someone else's work, stroke by stroke, and we erased and reworked. Many considered this to be a noncreative, harmful way to learn drawing. But we liked what we finally got. Our friends and classmates liked what we did and we were encouraged. We were on a roll, and that was of overriding importance.

Later we were able to learn technique, theory, media, and much more with the gift of incentive provided by friends, classmates, and family. Early on we copied, then we found ways to do our own original things.

Mimicry is prerequisite to creativity!

It is my hope that my readers will be able to come up with drawings that will bring them gratifying approval from friends, classmates, and family. After that I look forward to the competition.

Enjoy!

LEE J. AMES

DRAW
50 CREEPY
CRAWLIES

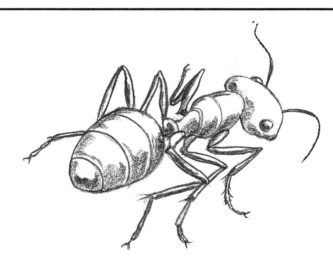

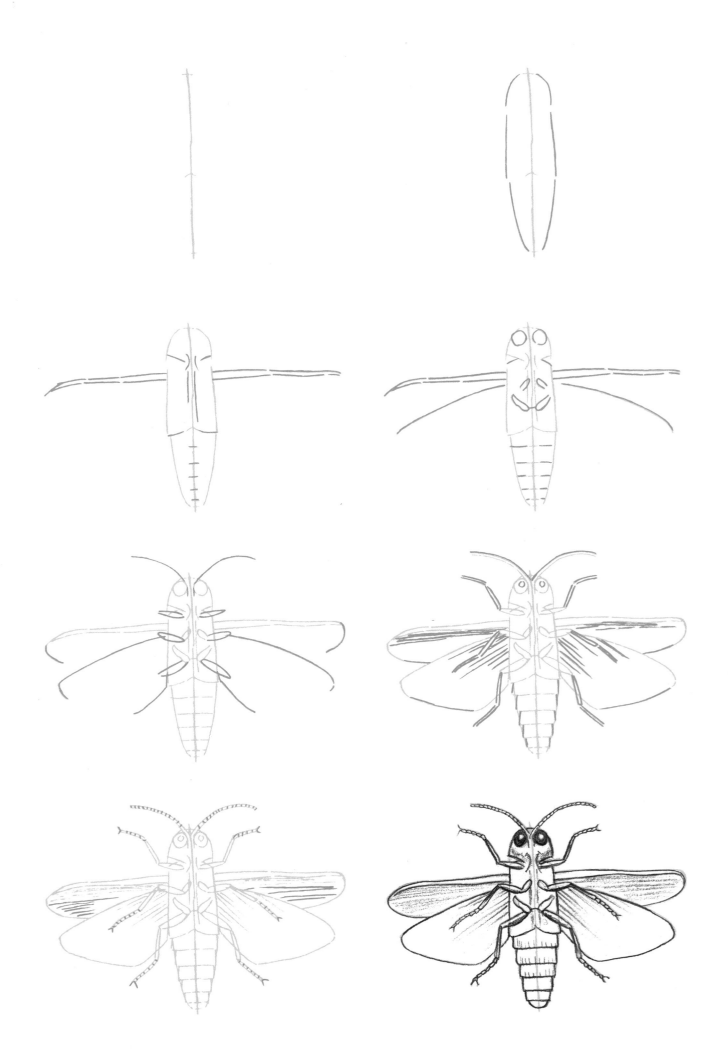

Firefly

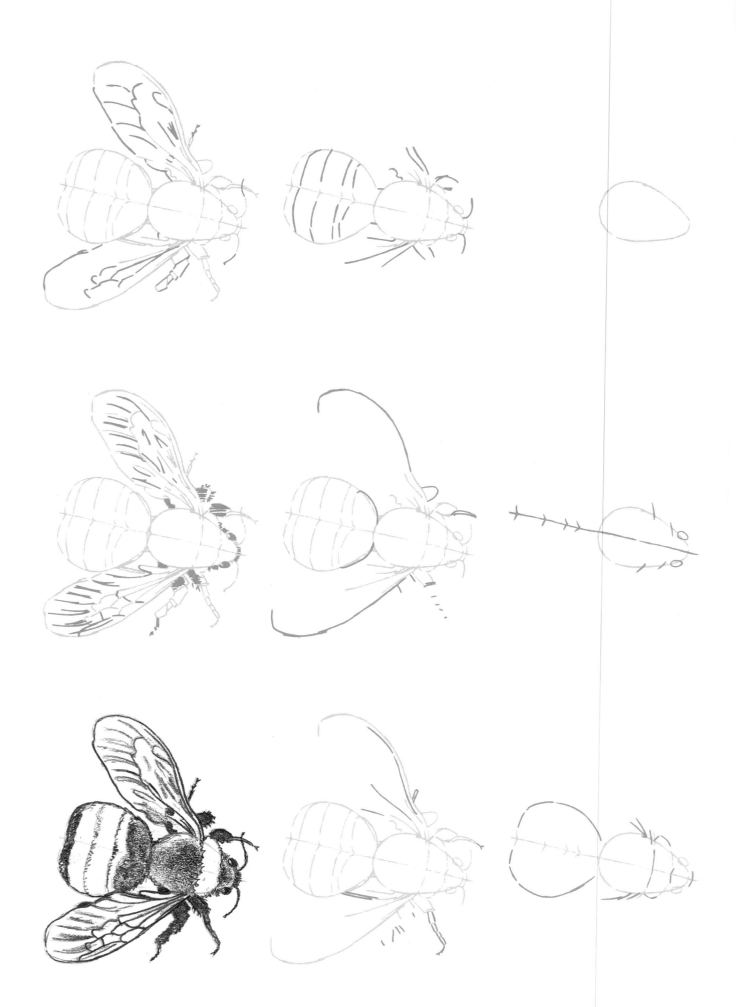

European Corn Borer Moth

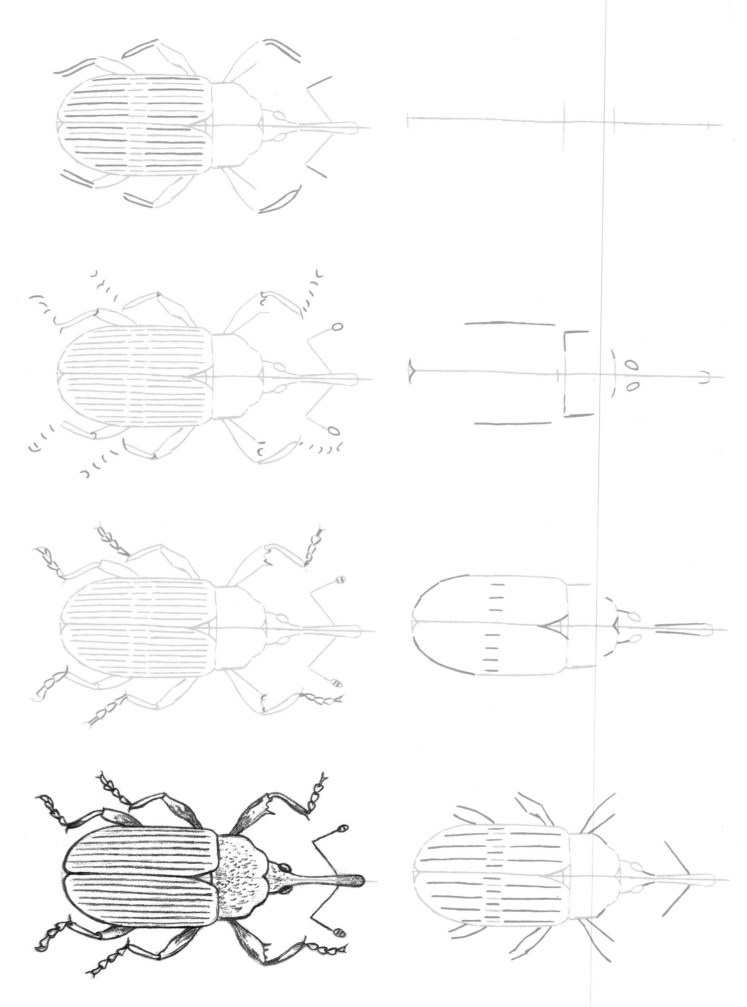

Boll Weevil

Winged Termite

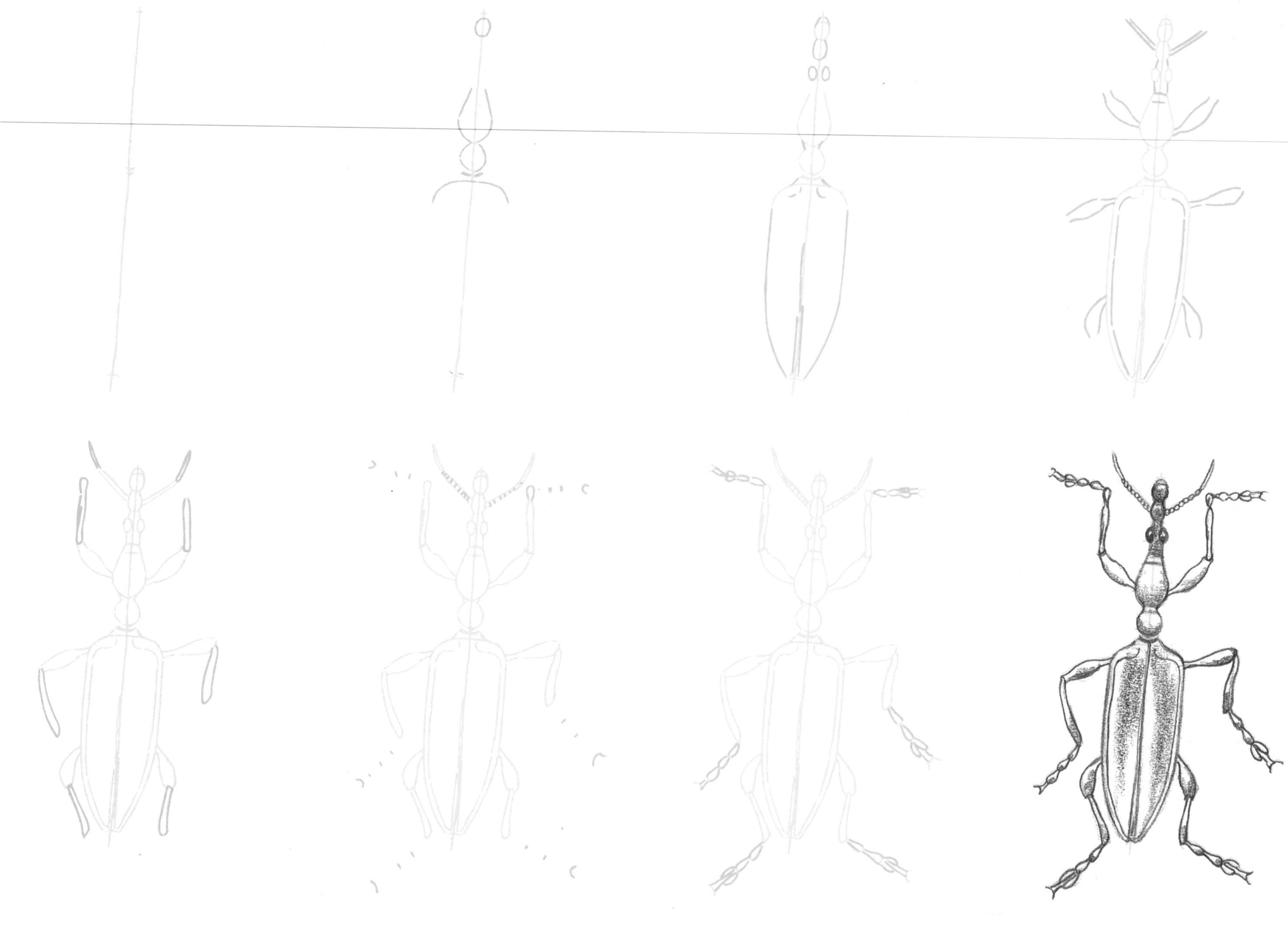

Sweet Potato Weevil

Japanese Beetle

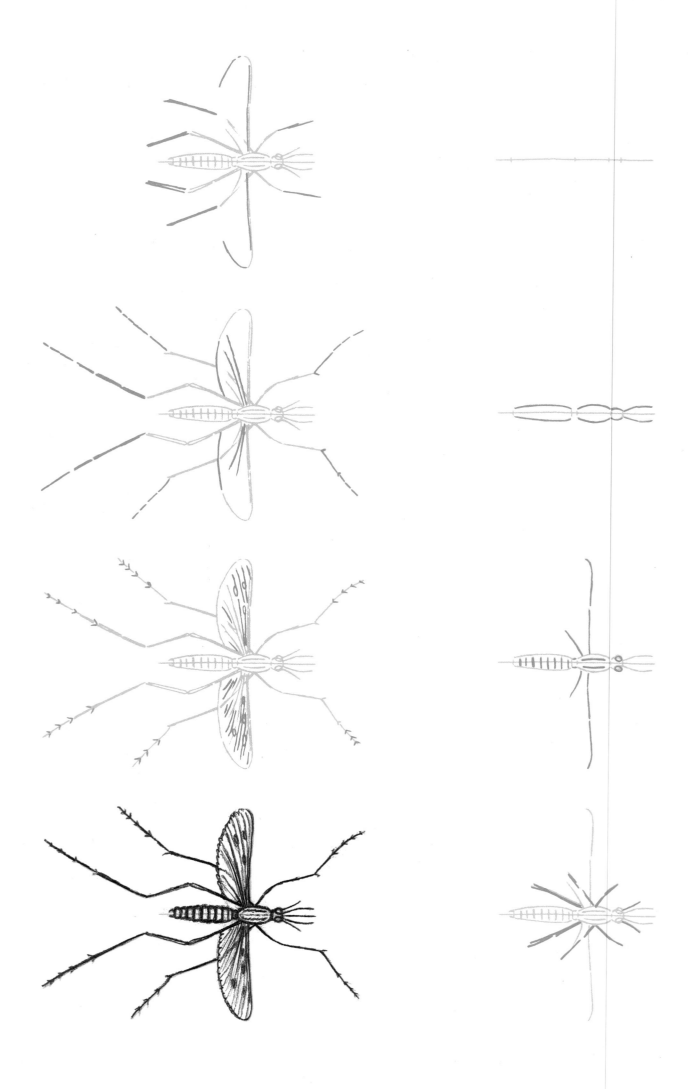

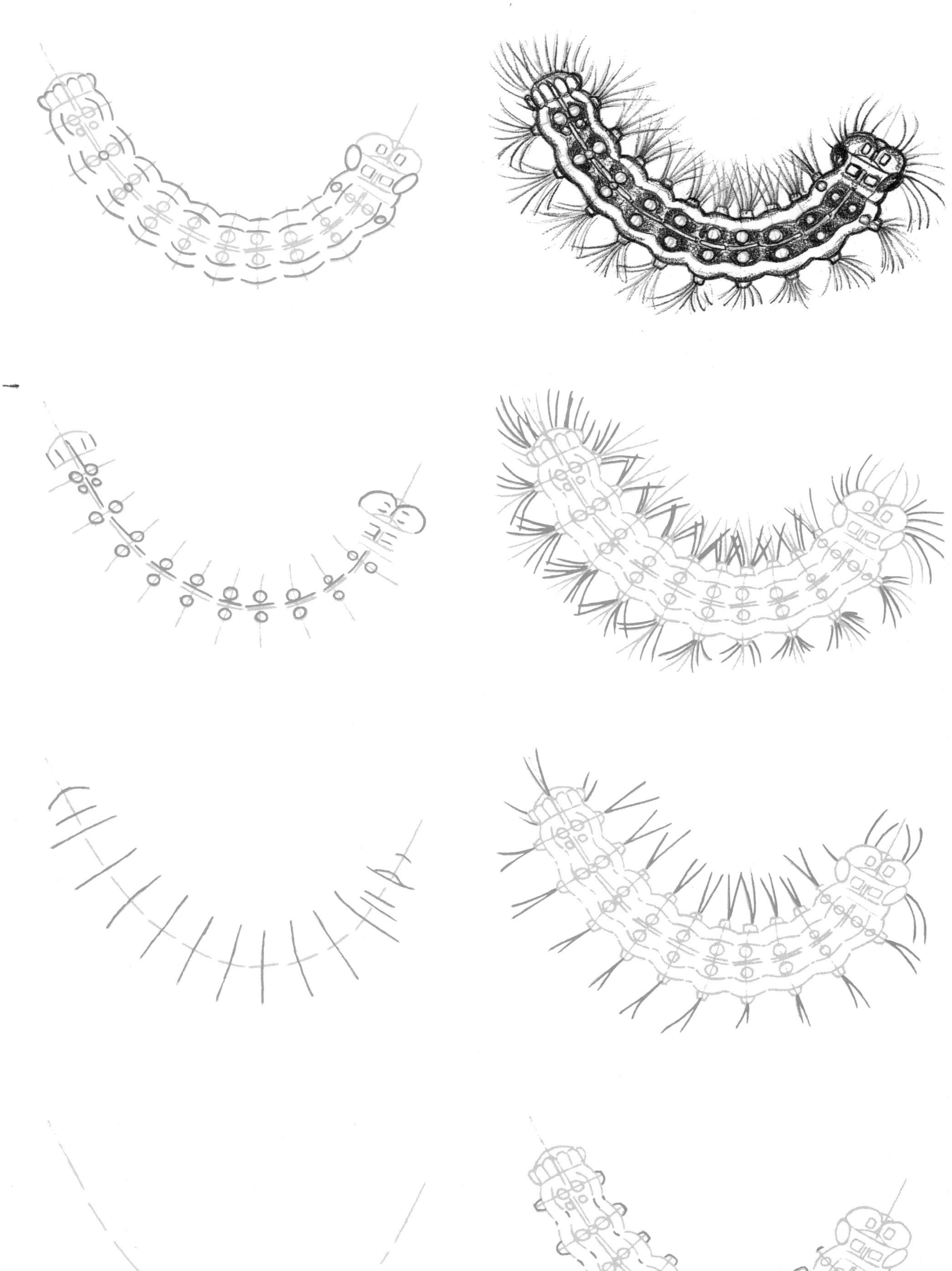

Gypsy Moth Larva

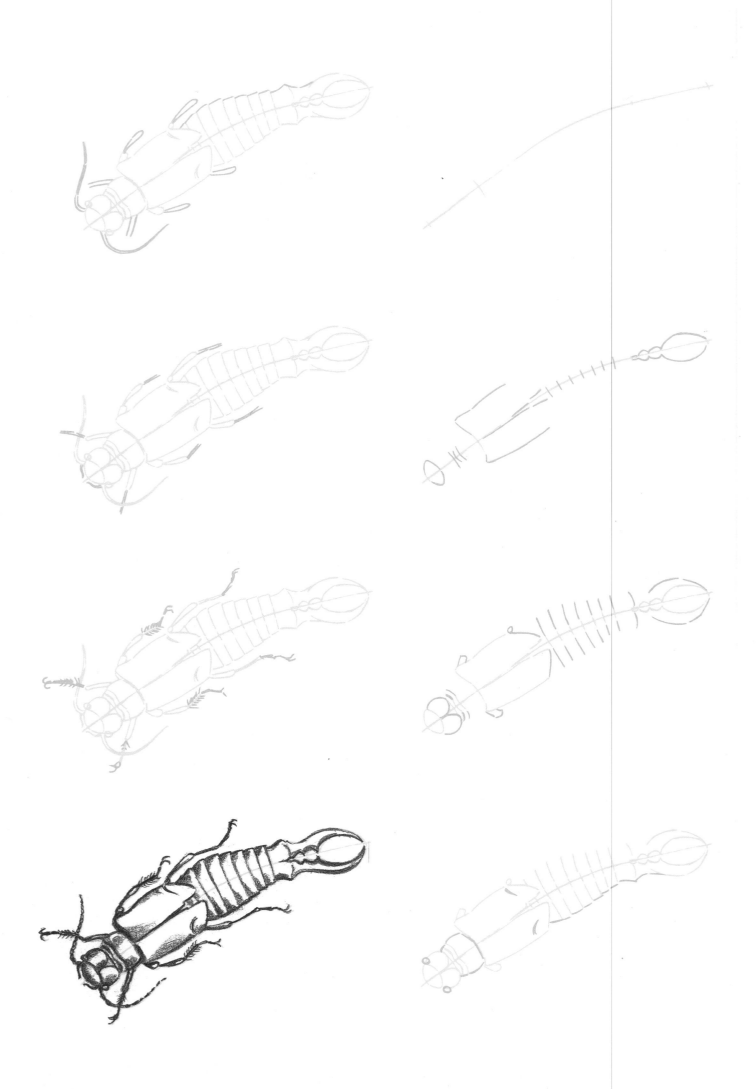

Earwig

Unicorn Beetle

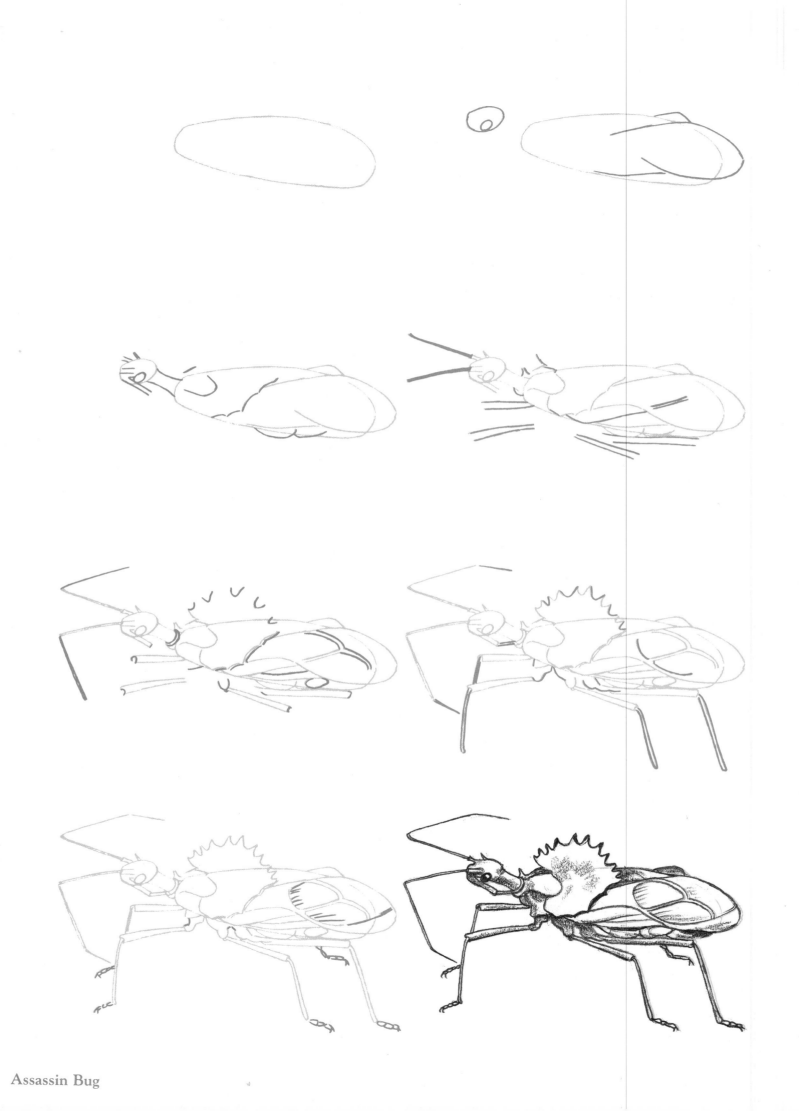

Assassin Bug

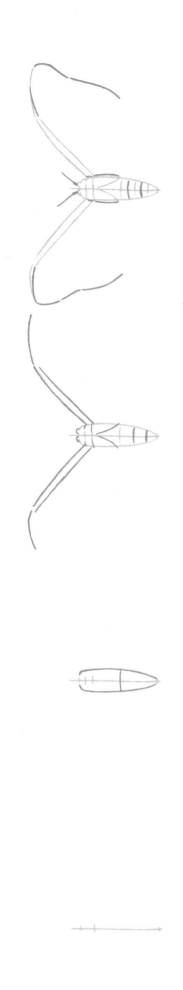

Walking Stick

Predacious Diving Beetle

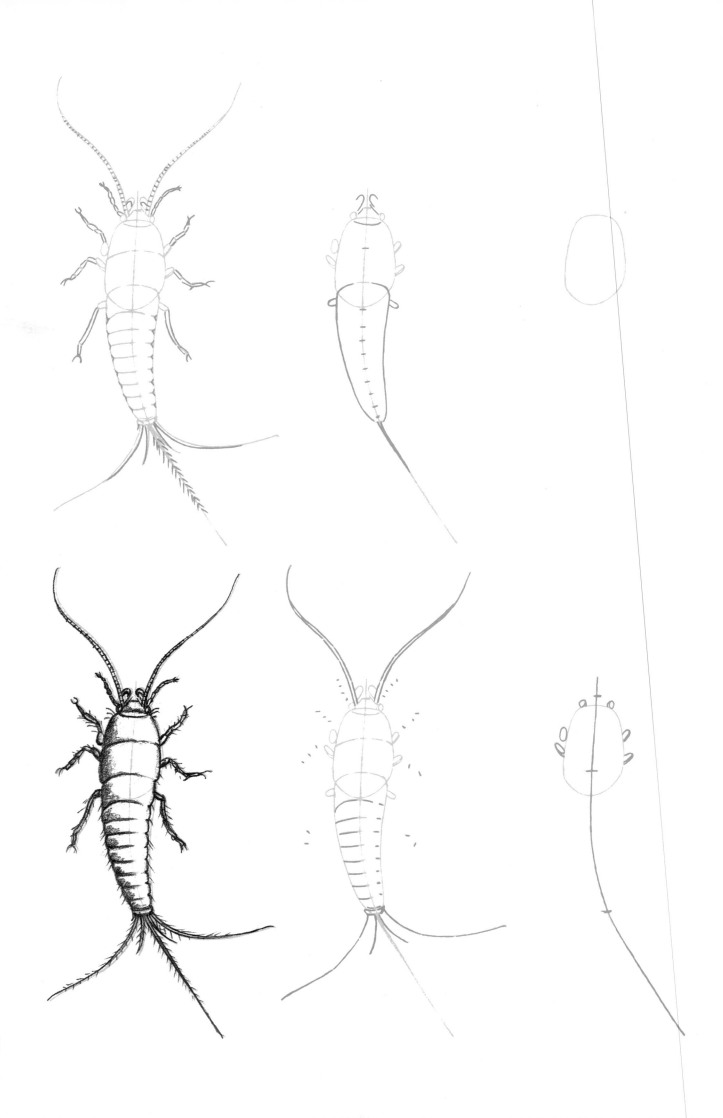

Silverfish

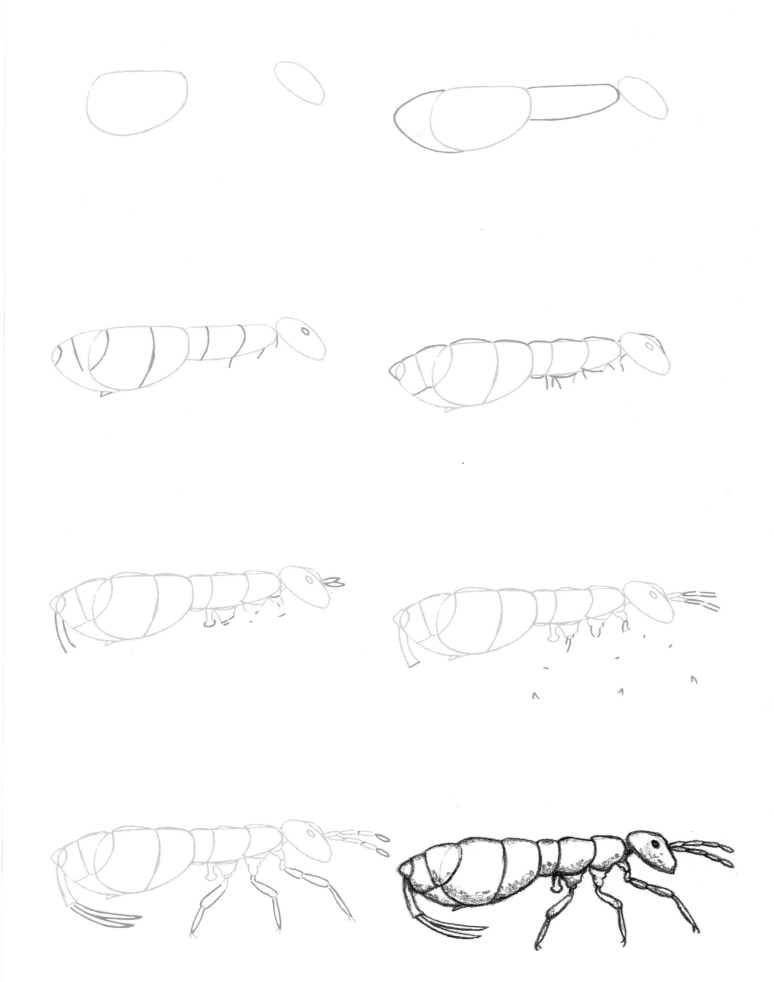

Springtail

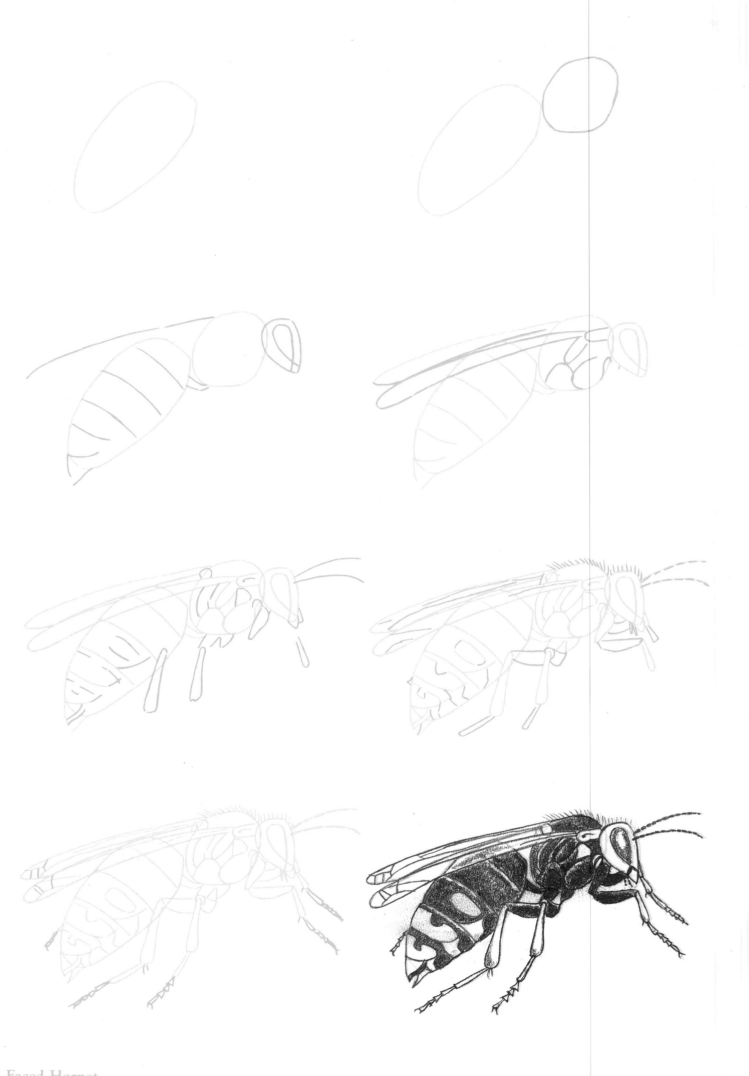

Bald-Faced Hornet

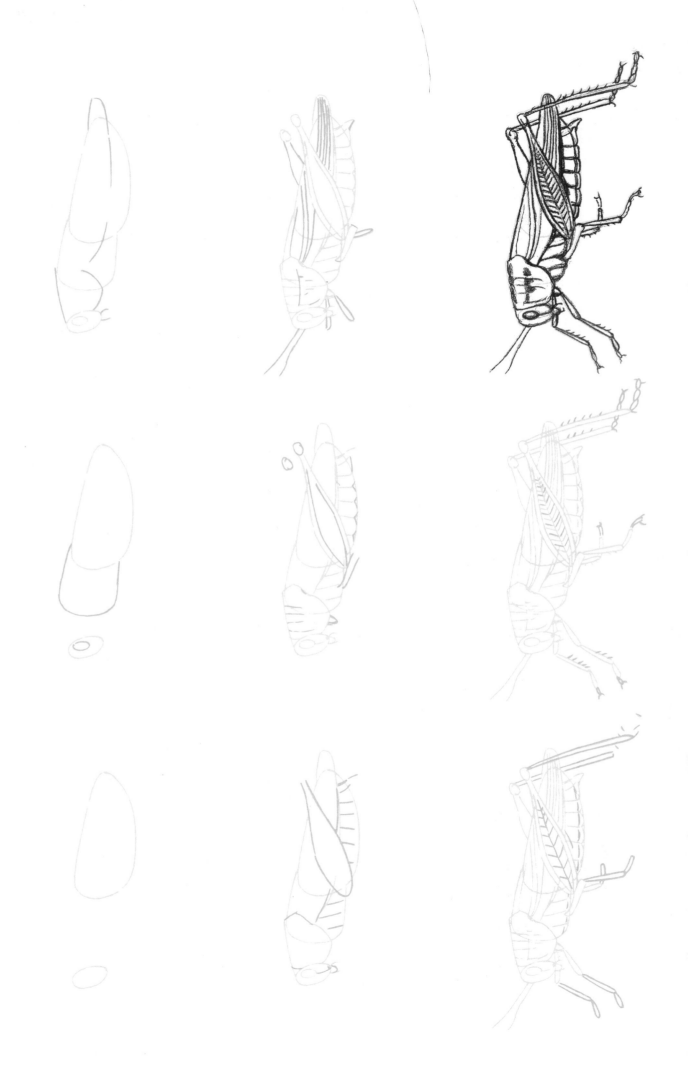

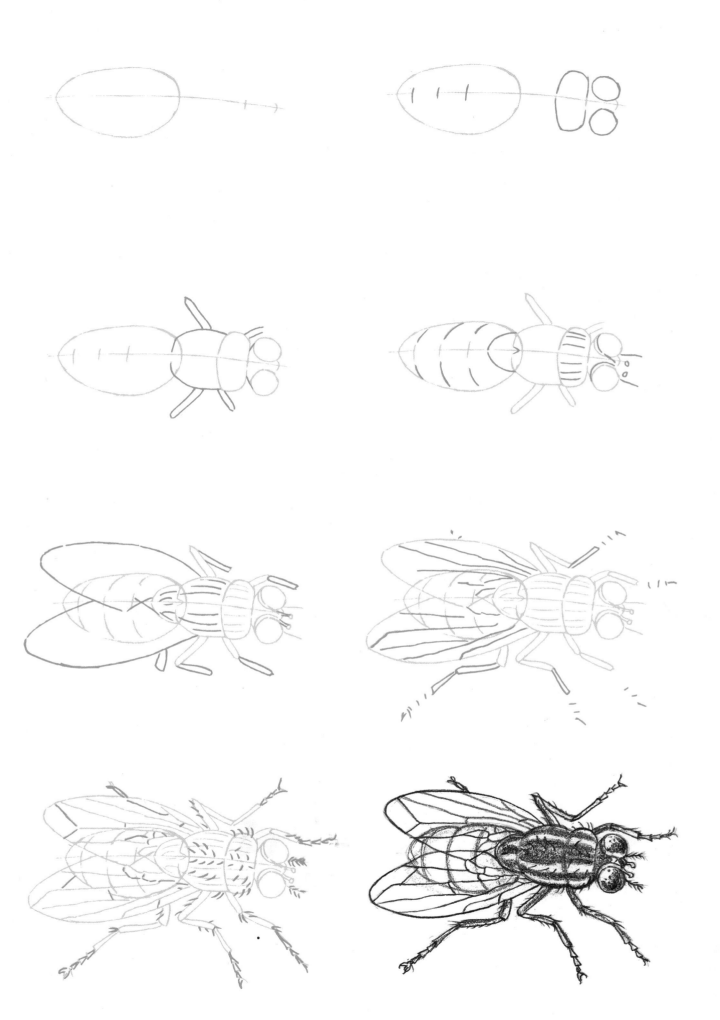

Housefly

American Cockroach

Army Worm

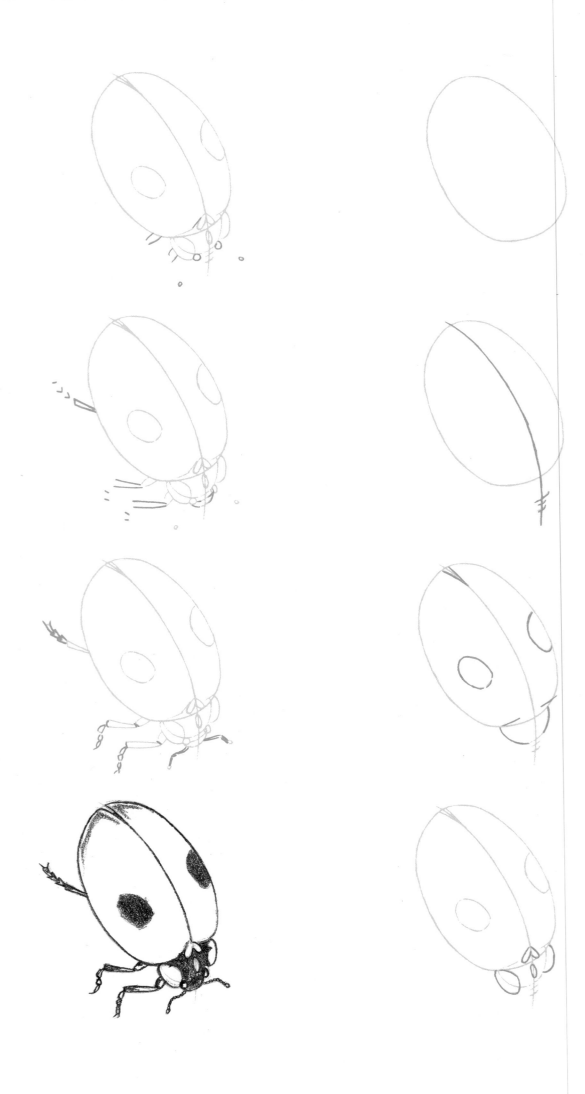

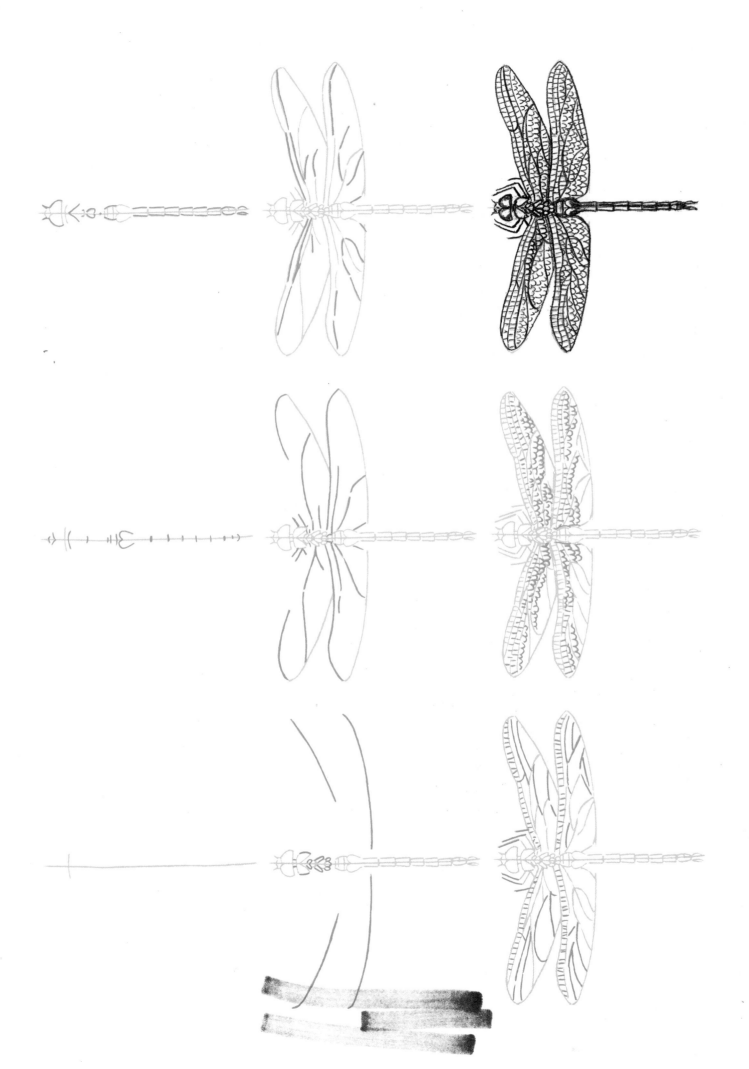

Bedbug

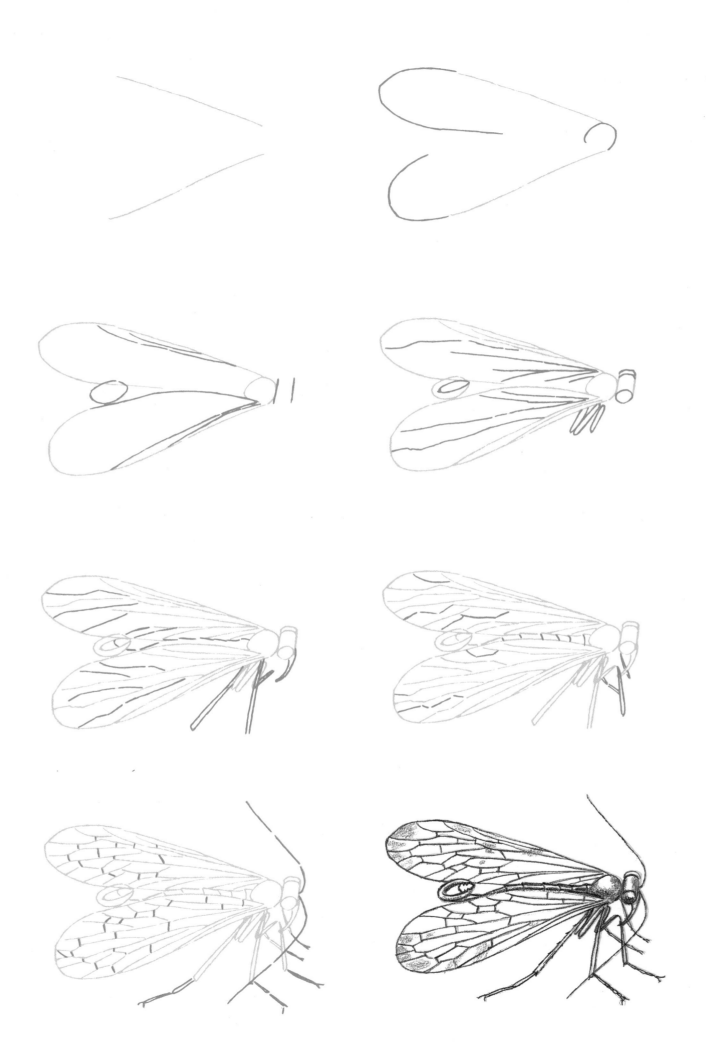

Scorpion Fly

Head Louse

Horntail

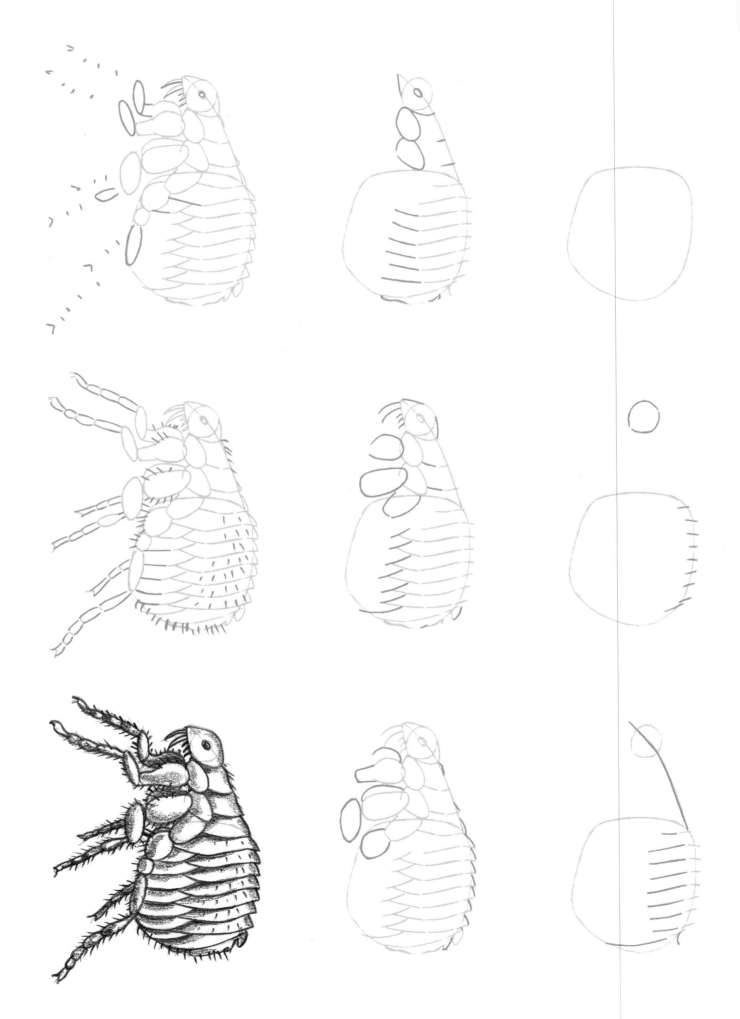

Dog Flea

Dung Beetle

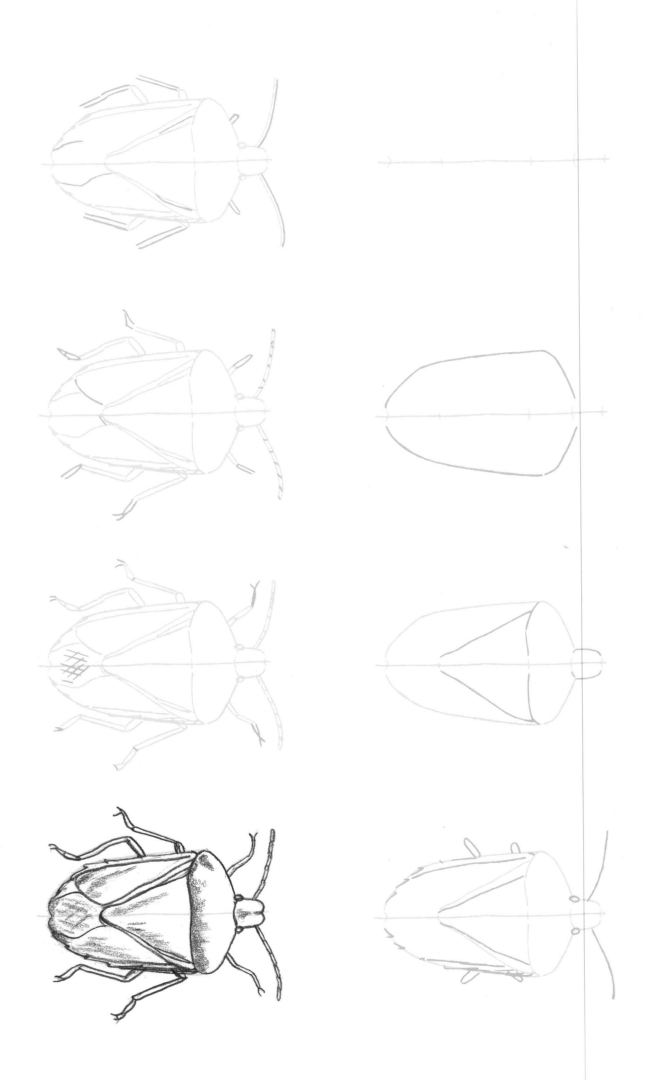

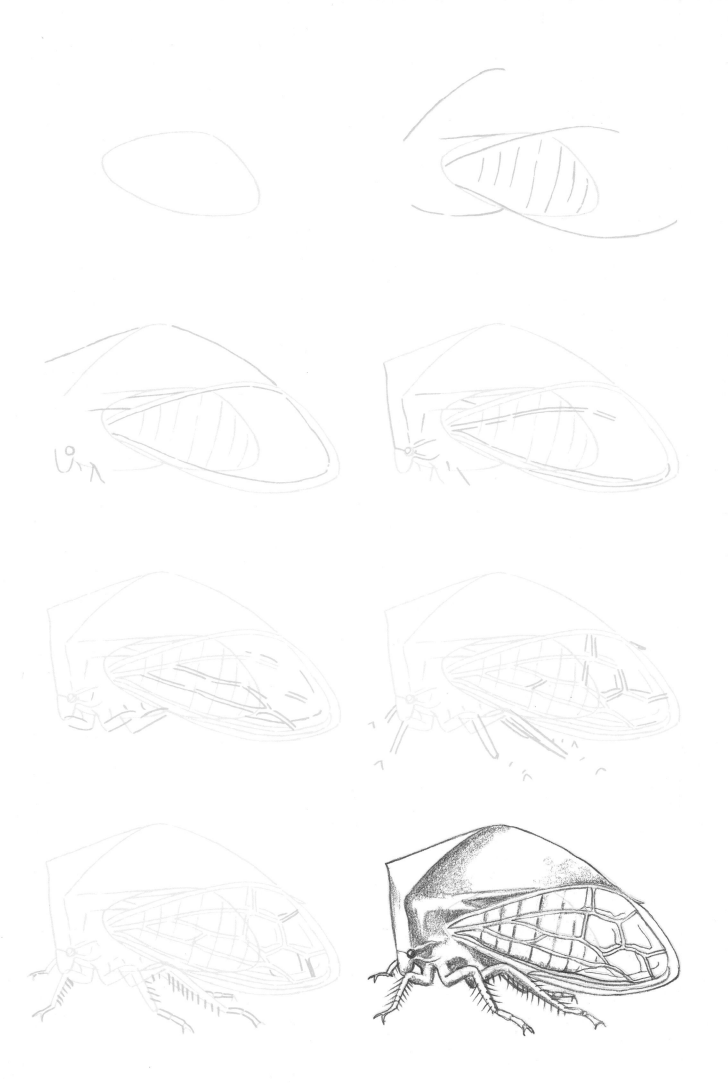

Buffalo Treehopper

Black Widow Spider

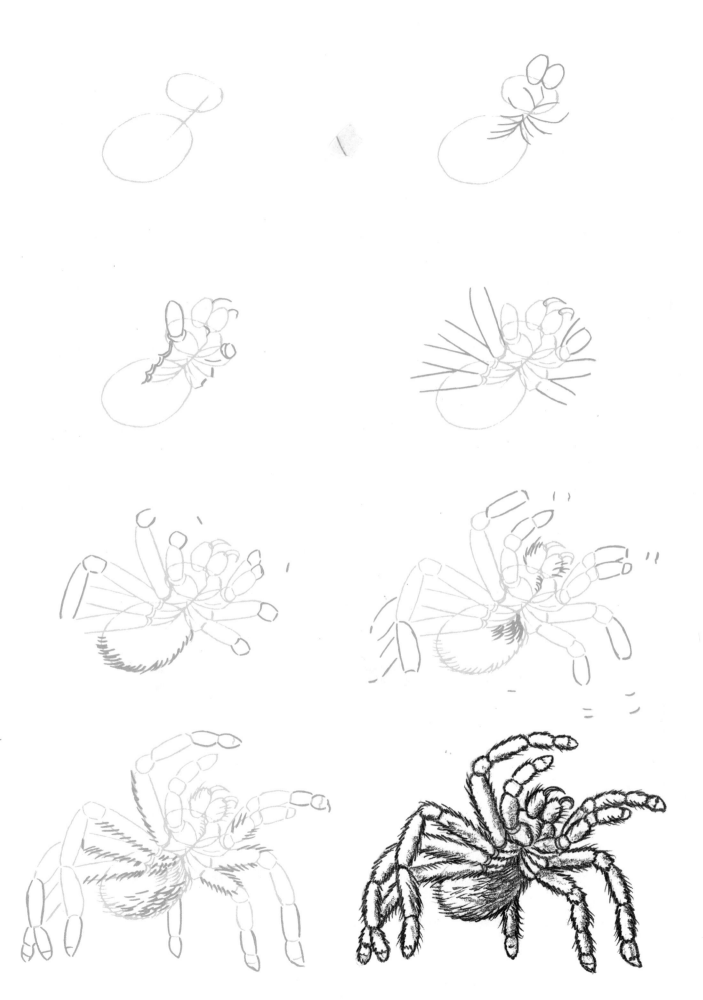

Tarantula

Wolf Spider

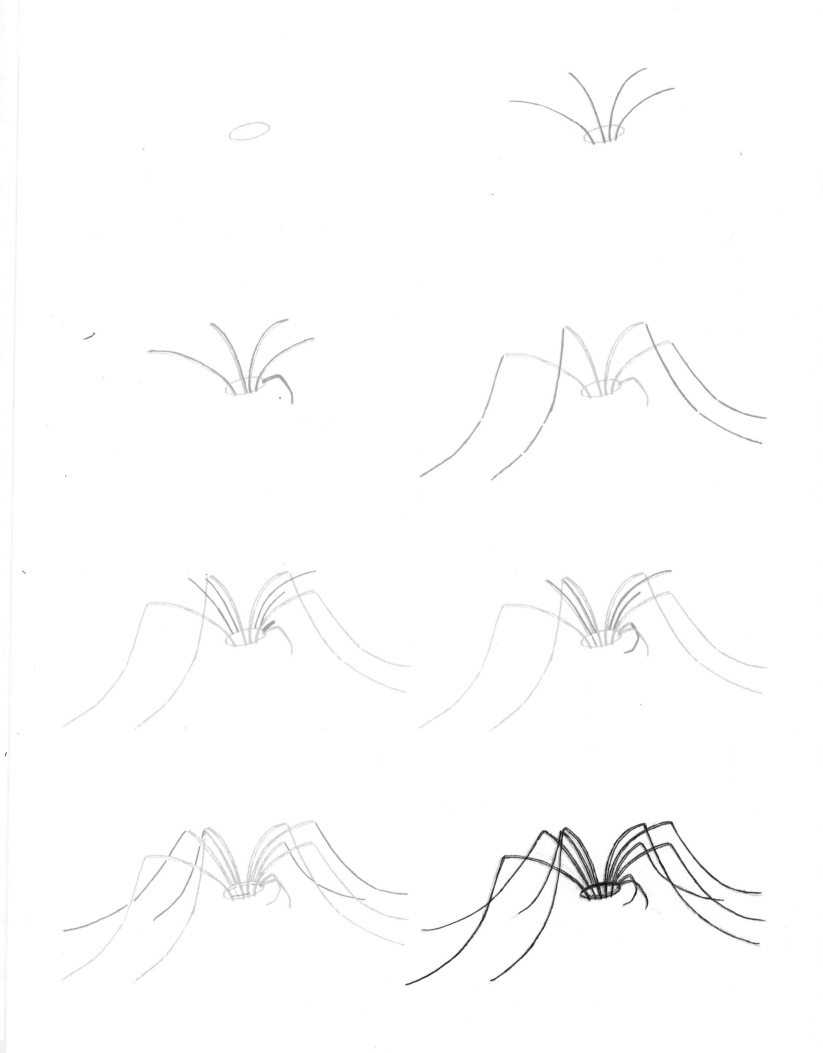

Daddy Longlegs

Slug

Snail

Scorpion

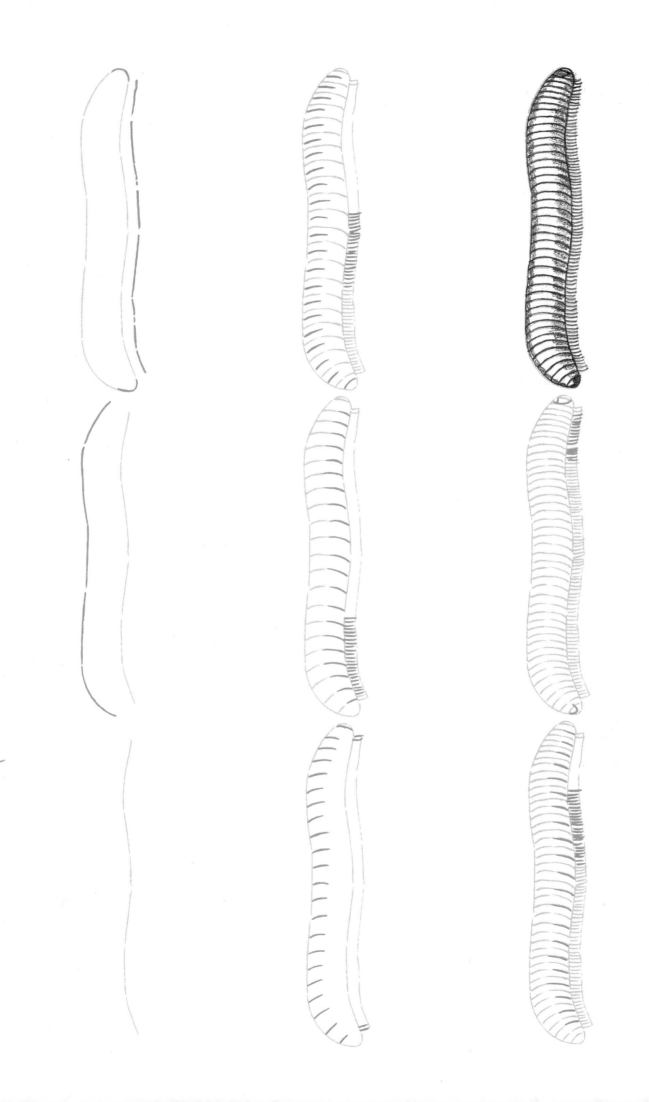

Millipede

Centipede

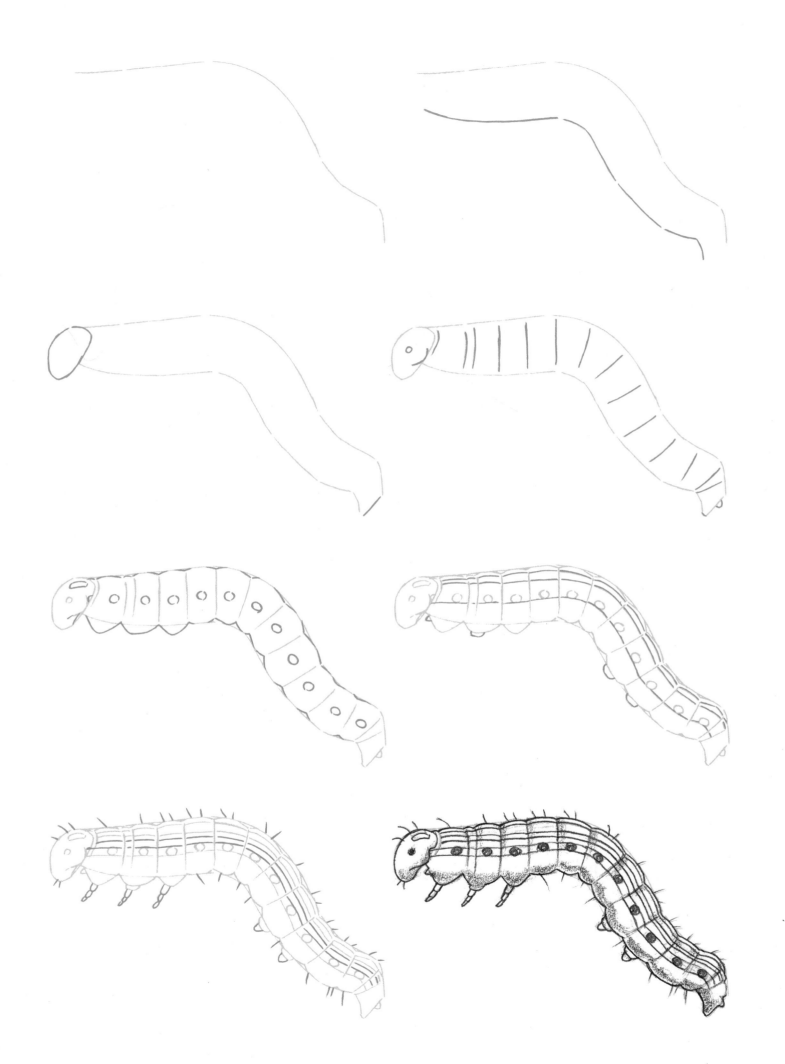

Caterpillar

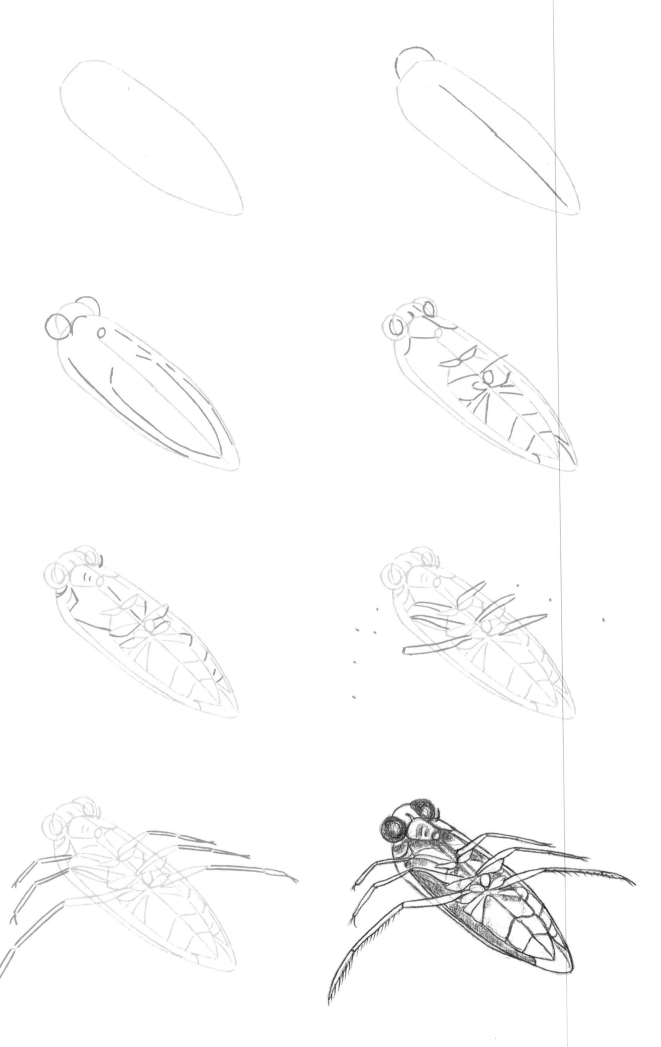

Back Swimmer

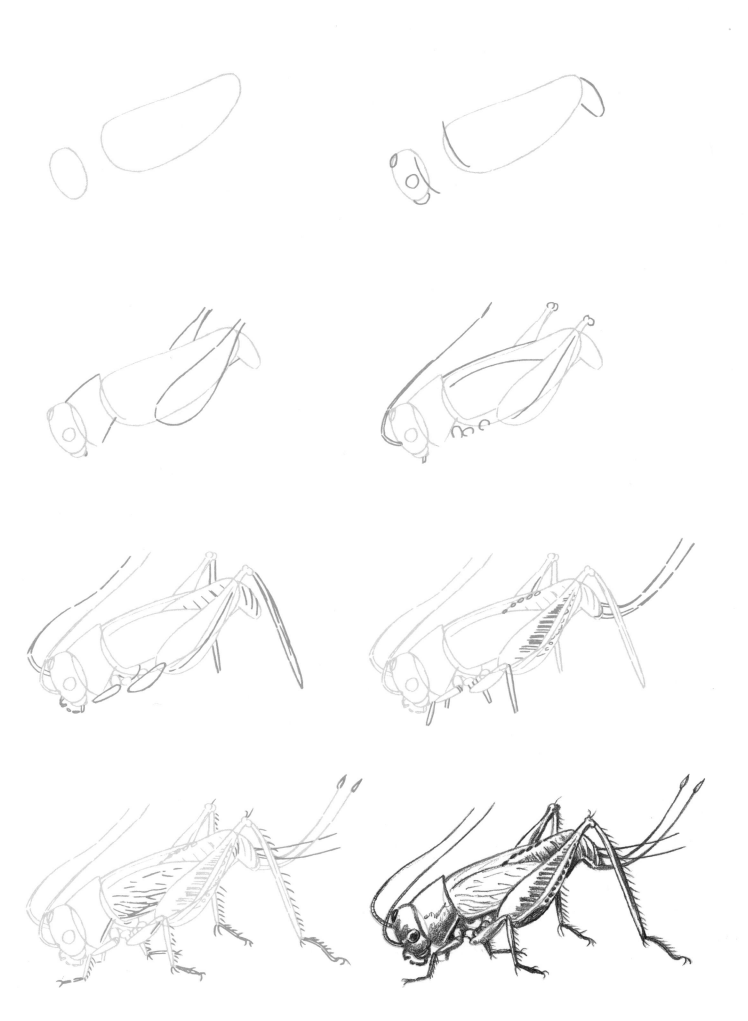

Field Cricket

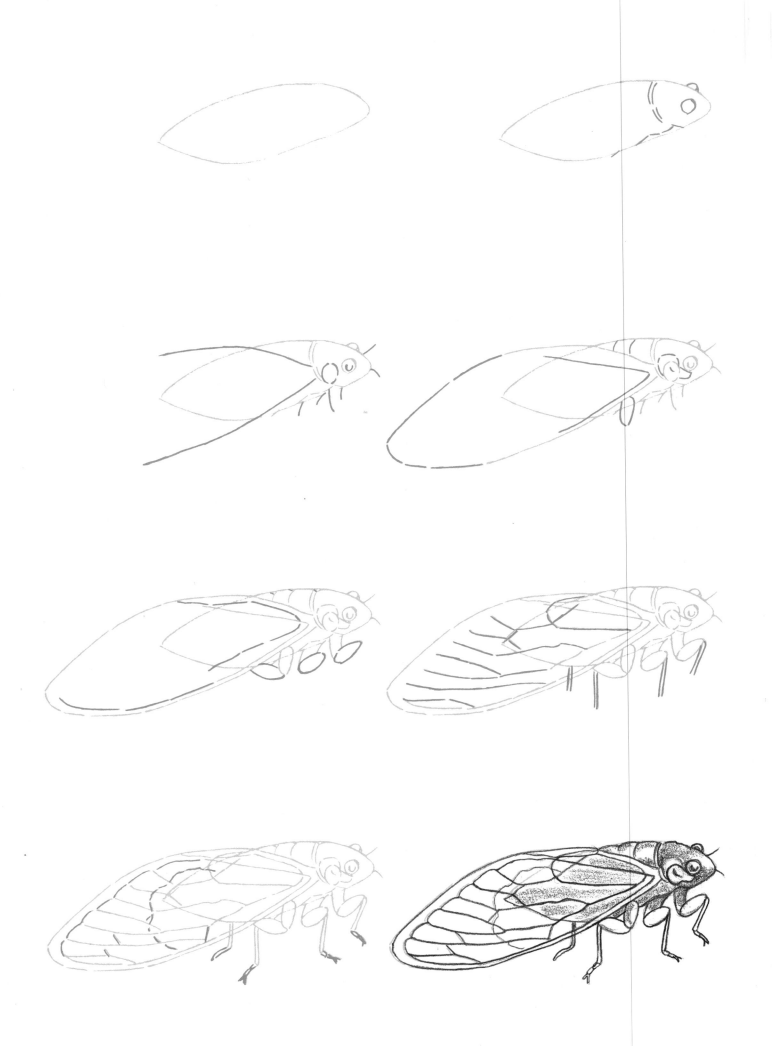

Cicada

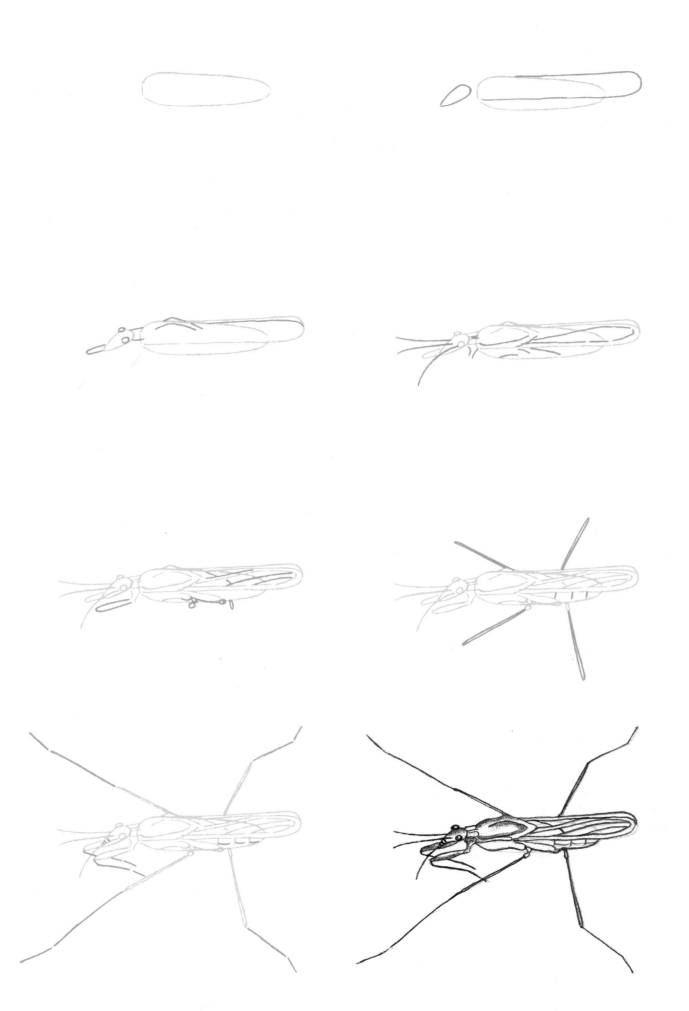

Water Strider

Lee J. Ames has been "drawing 50" since 1974, when the first "Draw 50" title—*Draw 50 Animals*—was published. Since that time, Ames has taught millions of people to draw everything from dinosaurs and sharks to boats, buildings, and cars. There are currently twenty titles in the "Draw 50" series, with nearly two million books sold.

Ames divides his time between Long Island, New York, where he runs an art studio, and Southern California. At the moment, he is working on a new drawing series for very young children.

Ray Burns has worked as a freelance illustrator since 1966. During that time he has illustrated close to seventy children's books, worked as a cartoonist, and created storyboards for television.

An ex-naval officer, Ray currently lives in Wilton, Connecticut, with his wife and their three children.